Jin Shin Jyutsu

Our hands, and feet are intelligent healers!
Simple hand & foot holds can help you feel better.

Jin Shin Jyutsu

literally translated is:

JIN - *Man of Knowing and Compassion*
SHIN - *Creator*
JYUTSU - *Art*

*Art of the Creator through
man of knowing and compassion*

written by Dianna L. Walker

Bowen practitioner of Australia;
Humans and Horses
Jin Shin Yyutsu, specializing in trauma release.

Inside this book

Information in this booklet is not intended as a replacement for medical diagnosis, consulting your medical care provider, or treatment. Dianna's personal experiences and beliefs find Jin Shin to be supportive of, and compatible with Medical practices and other Complementary approach. Nothing contained in this booklet is a substitute for diagnosis and treatment by your health-care provider.

JIN SHIN JYUTSU

Jin Shin Jyutsu is an art as opposed to a technique because a technique is a mechanical application, whereas an art is a skillful creation.

According to ancient written records, which remain in the Archives of the Imperial Palace in Japan, Jin Shin Jyutsu was widely known before the birth of Gautama (Buddha, India), before the birth of Moses (recorded in the Bible), and before the Kojiki (Record of Ancient Things - Japan, A.D. 712).

Jin Shin is the Art of releasing tensions which are the causes for various symptoms in the body. Our bodies contain several energy pathways that feed life into all of our cells. When one or more of these paths become blocked, this damming effect may lead to discomfort or even pain.

This stagnation will not only disrupt the local area but will continue and eventually disharmonize the complete path or paths of the energy flow.

Mary Burmeister, brought the Art from Japan to America in 1954. Her teachings, facilitated JSJ's awareness.

Jin Shin is noninvasive. Jin Shin practitioners employ the reading of energetic pulses to target imbalances in a body's energy patterns. When the Qi moves freely throughout the body, the body is in harmony. Blocked energy pathways cause physical, mental, or emotional disharmony, or "dis-ease" arises.

The Jin Shin touch is light, yet penetrating and supports the natural flow of the body's energy. Jin Shin utilizes the life force that emanates from our fingertips.

The practitioner merely touches, or connects two of the twenty-six energy release points and waits for the energy flow to correct itself. It helps everything from head to toe, and vice versa. There are 27 trillion cells in the body, and if we smile, all 27 trillion cells smile with us. The same principle is how we help ourselves in health.

Ones touch must be light enough that one could slide a piece of paper out from under both hands without displacing their position. Both the left hand and the right hand rest on the subject at the same time. Unlike other energy work, Jin Shin does not require any energy from the practitioner.

Eric Cuna

26 SEL ENERGY LOCKS
Safety Energy Locks

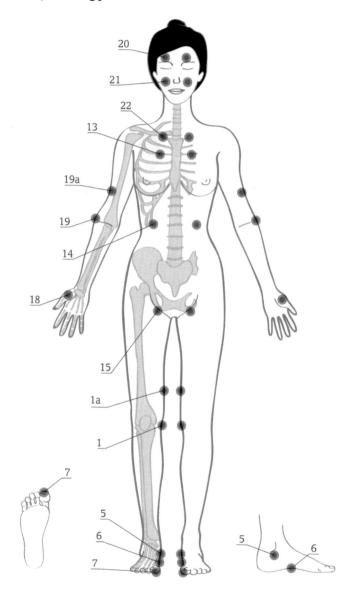

26 SEL ENERGY LOCKS
Safety Energy Locks

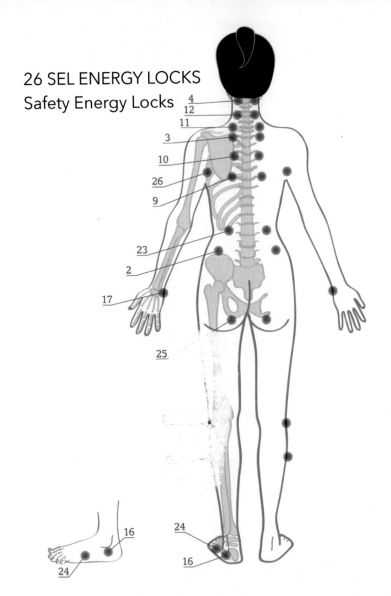

Each energy site will take seconds or minutes to release and reenergize. Use your left hand to lightly hold a finger on your right hand, then switch hands. Harmony is warmth and or tingling & eventually, synchronized pulses.

QUICK SELF HELP

Emotion or Malady   *Hand Holds*

When you feel confused
or you just cannot
remember

Place both hands on your
head

If you want to relax

Put your right hand on your
head
and Left hand on belly
button

You feel sad
You are worried

Hold your left hand thumb
in your right fingers

Then
Hold your right hand
thumb in your left fingers

When you have a *stomach ache*

Put one hand on your head and the other on your stomach

Or you can put both hands on your thighs

If you are *afraid*

Hold your pointer finger in left hand
Hold your pointer finger in right hand

When you are *Angry*

Hold your middle finger on your left hand
Hold your middle finger on your right hand

When you feel like crying

Hold your ring finger on
your right hand
Hold your ring finger on
your left hand

We all want to laugh

Hold your baby finger on
your left hand
Hold your baby finger on
your right hand

When you are tired

Sit on your hands for a few
minutes (about 20 minutes
is ideal)

When you are nauseous

Cross your hands and hold
SEL 1 at inner edge of
knees

When Grief strikes

Hold your ring finger

Hic
Hic
Hic
Hic

When you have Hiccups

Hold area just behind
earlobes at SEL 12
at right side of base
of neck

Insomnia

Hold the base of the thumb at SEL 18 at palm side of base of thumb

For ongoing anxiety

Cross arms at the chest. Place right hand in left armpit, and left and at crux of thumb in right armpit

Exhaustion, mental confusion, eye strain, cramping and increase foot circulation.

Place palms of hand together; fingertips to wrist.

Cradle your foot in your hand; (left foot with left hand) Thumb is holding top of foot, and fingers touch center of sole

Fainting

Hold base of skull at SEL 4

Back of head headache

Hold thumb at SEL 18

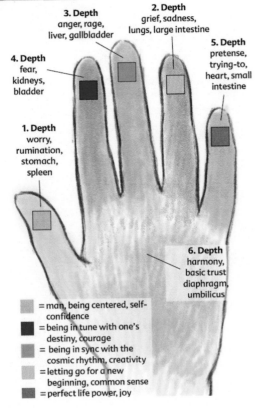

3. Depth
anger, rage,
liver, gallbladder

2. Depth
grief, sadness,
lungs, large intestine

5. Depth
pretense,
trying-to,
heart, small
intestine

4. Depth
fear,
kidneys,
bladder

1. Depth
worry,
rumination,
stomach,
spleen

6. Depth
harmony,
basic trust
diaphragm,
umbilicus

= man, being centered, self-confidence
= being in tune with one's destiny, courage
= being in sync with the cosmic rhythm, creativity
= letting go for a new beginning, common sense
= perfect life power, joy

Aids in revitalization of all bodily functions.
Releases blockages that lead to daily fatigue.

Before you begin:
Ask yourself:

- Bad complexion?
- Temperamental and cannot help it?
- Uncontrollable craving for sweets?
- Nothing is wrong, but I am tried always.
- I have uneasy feelings.

Make a circle with the right middle finger and thumb.
Do this by placing the palm side of the thumb on the
middle fingernail.

Then slip the left thumb between the circle of the right
thumb and middle finger.

Calm & Revitalize

Before you begin:

- Do you get nervous?
- Worry about your heart?
- Walked very little and became out of breath?
- Get depressed & never seem to have fun?

Hold the palm side of the left little and ring fingers with the right thumb. Place the other right fingers on the back of the left little and ringer fingers.

Remember to reverse and hold right little finger and ring fingers with the left thumb.

This calls the body, releases nervous tension and stress and revitalizes all of the organ functions

Harmonizing the Main Central regularly helps you feel centered and ensures that you will have plenty of energy. Some people find it calming and use it to fall asleep, while others like to use it to clear away the cobwebs upon awakening. For optimum results, do this daily.

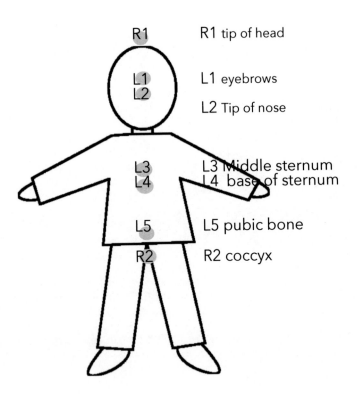

R1 tip of head

L1 eyebrows

L2 Tip of nose

L3 Middle sternum

L4 base of sternum

L5 pubic bone

R2 coccyx

*Main source of
energy sequence*

Step 1: Place the fingers of the right hand on the top of the head (where they will remain until step 6). Place the fingers of the left hand on your forehead between your eyebrows. Hold for 2 to 5 minutes or until the pulses you feel at your fingertips synchronize with each other.

Step 2: Now move the left fingertips to the tip of the nose. Hold them there for 2 to 5 minutes, or until the pulses synchronize.

Step 3: Move the left fingertips to your sternum)center of your chest between your breasts).

Stay there for 2 to 5 minutes or until the pulses synchronize.

Step 4: Move your fingers to the base of your sternum (center of where your ribs start, above the stomach). Hold them there for 2 to 5 minutes, or until the pulses synchronize

Step 5: Move your fingers to the top of your pubic bone (above the genitals, center). Stay there for 2 to 5 minutes, or until the pulses synchronize.

Step 6: Keep your left fingertips in place and move your right fingertips to cover your coccyx (tailbone). Hold for 2 to 5 minutes or until the pulses you feel at your fingertips synchronize with each other.

Note: The right hand remains on the top of the head while the left hand moves down the body until the final step.

Jin Shin Jyutsu

HANDS & FEET

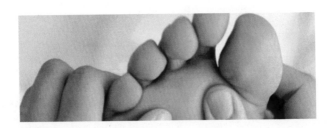

If your head hurts

Hold Big toe on Right foot
Hold Big toe on Left foot
Now you can think and
remember too!!

If your eyes hurt

On your Right foot hold
your first toe.
As your eyes feel better,
hold your first toe on Left
foot.

If your back hurts

Hold your Right baby toe
then,
Hold your Left baby toe

Cancer
Radiation & Chemotherapy

Possible Side Effects -

Fatigue

During Chemotherapy & Radiation Therapy, fatigue may set in, and can last long after the completion of the treatments.

Cancer cells die off as a result of the treatments and create waste, which is then eliminated by the kidneys. Fatigue is caused when the kidneys are overworked and have to work twice as hard to cope with this destruction. This can give rise to feelings of frustration and inability to cope, when we do not understand what is happening.

To support Kidney energy.

• Place Right hand on Pubic bone and Left hand holds Right little toe. OR hold your Index finger for a few minutes until harmonized. Reverse for Left side.

• The Liver becomes overworked as it makes new blood cells, and give nourishment to provide energy and support for the body.

To support Liver energy.

• *Place Right hand on Right Safety Energy Lock 4 and Left hand on Left Safety Energy Lock 22 for a few minutes. (Reverse for Left side). Or hold Left and Right Safety Energy Lock 4 at the same time (Left hand on Left, Right hand on Right).*

Depression

When sad thoughts burden us they may disrupt the energy of the stomach and large intestine, and may contribute to depression.

- To re-harmonize the energies of both these organs, simply give yourself a big hug, by crossing your arms and placing your fingers under your armpits.
- Exhale and Inhale while holding these points for 36 breaths or till you feel calm and secure.
- Hold your Left thumb with your Right hand then your ring finger with your Right hand for a few minutes.
- Then hold your Right thumb with your Left hand then hold your Right ring finger with your Left hand for a few minutes.

These holds have the potential to soothe and uplift you.

Lymphedema

Lymphedema is the swelling of the soft tissues caused by a build up of lymph fluid. It can occur in the hand, arm, breast, trunk, abdomen or leg. To help all of the above:

- Place your Right thumb in the centre of the Left armpit and wrap your fingers around the top of Left arm.
- Hold opposite inner thigh with Left hand. Lymphedema occurring in the arm or hand.
- Hold Safety Energy Lock 26 (see page 6), on the side of the affected arm with opposite hand, and place the end of the thumb over the nail of the ring finger (creating a circle).
- Hold for 20 minutes or longer, and you may begin to feel the arm pumping upwards.

Nausea

Hold the wrist at Safety Energy Lock 17 and / or Safety Energy Lock 18 till nausea ceases.

Toxic Headaches

- Hold both big toes (Safety Energy Lock 7) until pain subsides.

Heartburn

- Place Right hand (fingers pointing towards head) between Safety Energy Lock 13 (see page 6) on Sternum.
- Place Left hand between Safety Energy Locks 14 (base of Rib cage), fingers pointing downwards.
- Reverse for other side. Hold for a few minutes.

Constipation or Diarrhea

- Place one hand on Coccyx and the other hand on the outside of the knee at Safety Energy Lock 8 (see page 6).
- Hold for 15 minutes.
- Or hold Index finger, then Ring finger for 3-5 minutes on each finger.

Remember.....

"Make changes in your life. Smile."
"Change focus. Change thoughts"
"Every breath, well lived, makes yesterday a dream of
happiness, and tomorrow ecstasy."
"Lovingly hold fingers."
"Drop the shoulders and exhale. Focus on harmony, not
disharmony." "Perfect. Everyday I am perfect."

A compilation by Lynne Pflueger & Michael Wenninger.

Notes

Notes

Notes

Cowell Family Cancer Center

I am more than my body,
I am more than my mind,
I am a Spirit,
I am Divine

Many thanks to the Cowell Family Cancer Center for providing the funds to print this book.

The Health and Wellness Suite offers:

Art and Music Therapy
Essentials Boutique
Yoga
Integrative Therapies: Bowen from Australia, Acupuncture, Zen Shiatsu, Massage.
Nutrition help
Resources and Learning Center
Stress Reduction and Spiritual Health
Meditation
Support Groups

Feel free to drop by anytime!

217 S. Madison St.
Traverse City, MI 49684
(231) 392-8400
cancerservices@mhc.net

MUNSON MEDICAL CENTER
MUNSON HEALTHCARE

Made in the USA
Lexington, KY
14 May 2019